SECOND EDITION

Storybook 12

The Car Book

by Sue Dickson

Illustrations by Norma Portadino, Jean Hamilton, Chip Neville and Kerstin Upmeyer

Printed in the United States of America

Modern Curriculum Press, an imprint of Pearson Learning
299 Jefferson Road, P.O. Box 480, Parsippany, NJ 07054
1-800-321-3106 / www.pearsonlearning.com

ISBN: 1-56704-522-7 (Volume 12)

H I J K L M N—CJK—05

D0171421

Table of Contents

Raceway Step 25

Harmony Hill Farm

Vocabulary

1. farm
2. Mark
3. Carl
4. Sparky
5. barn
6. arf arf
7. bark
8. barked
9. lark
10. large
11. cart
12. yard
13. yards
14. jar
15. star
16. stars
17. dark
18. Marcy
19. sharp
20. yarn
21. artist
22. far
23. Mars
24. charm
25. hard
26. garden
27. arm
28. arm ful
    armful
29. Martha
30. barn yard
    barnyard
31. harm
32. dart
33. darted
34. smart
35. harp
36. park

3

This is Harmony Hill
Farm. Carl and Mark
live here. They like
Harmony Hill Farm.

4

Mark is big. He is seven years old. Carl is not so big. He is five years old.

Mark has a little puppy.
His name is Sparky.

"Here Sparky," said
Mark. "Let's go help
Dad. He is at the barn."

Mark ran to the barn
and Sparky ran with him.

"Arf, arf !" barked
Sparky.

Mark looked up in the tree by the barn. He saw a lark sitting on a branch.

"Tweet, tweet," went the lark.

"Good morning to you, too," said Mark.

8

"Hi, Dad," said Mark.

"Good morning, Mark," said Dad. Dad had a large fork. He was lifting hay into a cart.

"May I help you, Dad ?" asked Mark.

"Yes, you may help me," said Dad. "Here is an armful of hay for Old Martha."

Mark liked to feed Old Martha. He saw her by the fence in the barnyard.

10

Mark dropped the hay by Old Martha. Sparky ran up to her and barked.

"Arf, arf!" went Sparky.

Old Martha saw Sparky's sharp teeth. She did not like Sparky in her yard. "Moo!" went Old Martha.

"Come away, Sparky," said
Mark. "Come away with
me. Old Martha wants to
eat the hay. Do not harm
her."

Sparky darted out of the
barnyard with a bark. "Arf,
arf!" went Sparky.

"You are smart!" said
Mark.

Mark ran in to see his mom. She was dusting her harp. It was a large gold harp. Mom liked to play it.

"Mom is smart, too," said Mark.

"Arf, arf !" barked Sparky.

Twinkle twinkle little star, how I wonder what you are . . .

Carl ran in to see Mom.

"Mom, Mom!" said Carl. "May I go to the park? Mark can go with me. I want to catch bugs. I will help Mark catch some, too. We will keep them in a jar."

14

"Yes, Carl," said Mom. "You and Mark may go to the park. Take Sparky with you, too. Come home before dark."

"We will be back by dark," said Mark. "We want to see <u>Stars and Planets</u> on TV. It starts at six o'clock. We do not want to miss it."

"Very well," said Mom.
"I will see you at six
o'clock. Do not forget the
jars for your bugs."

Carl and Mark went to the park. Sparky went with them.

Carl got six bugs. He put them in his jar.

Mark got seven bugs. He put them in his jar. "See my large bugs !" said Mark.

18

Miss Marcy Sharp sat in the park. Sparky ran up to her.

"Arf, arf!" went Sparky.

Miss Marcy Sharp had red yarn in her basket. Sparky barked at it. Then, with a quick nip, off he ran with the yarn!

"No !" yelled Miss Marcy Sharp. "Come back with my yarn ! You are a bad dog !"

Carl and Mark ran to catch Sparky !

On and on Sparky ran
in the park. He ran past
an artist. He ran fast
with the red yarn.

Sparky ran to some
little kids. They had cars
and trucks in the sand.
They did not stop Sparky.
He ran on and on !

At last Mark and Carl got Sparky. Mark had to roll up the red yarn.

Wow! I bet I wound up five hundred yards!

Carl gave the yarn to Miss Marcy Sharp.

"Thank you," she said.

"I hope the yarn isn't a darker shade of red now," said Carl.

"It looks fine to me," said Miss Marcy Sharp.

"We must go home," said Carl to Mark. "It will be dark soon."

"<u>Stars and Planets</u> is on," said Mom, as Mark and Carl came in. A rocket whizzed by the stars to Mars on the TV screen. It went far, far up into the sky.

25

"I would not want to go to Mars," said Mark. "I like Harmony Hill Farm. I like our garden and barn. I like the lark in the tree by the barn. I like the hay cart. I like Old Martha in the barnyard."

"And Sparky !" said Carl.

"Yes, Harmony Hill Farm
has a lot of charm,
starting with my Mark
and Carl !" said Mom.
Then Mom hugged them
both hard in her arms.

The End

A Fawn at Dawn
A Rhyming Tale

Vocabulary

1. dawn		12. flaw
2. fawn		13. jaw
3. yawn		14. jaws
4. yawned		15. claws
5. crawl		
6. crawled		**Story Words**
7. paw		16. head
8. straw		17. other
9. lawn		an other
10. hawk		18. another
11. law		19. another's
		20. Mother Nature

At dawn, a fawn crawled out of bed.

He yawned and raised his sleepy head.

He slowly stamped each little paw
To get off every bit of straw.

He went ten steps
across the lawn
And nibbled apples
with a yawn.

Next, he saw a little mouse

Running quickly to its house.

Will that hawk with sharp, sharp claws

Catch that mouse with its big jaws ?

Oh dear !

Hurry !

The fawn was glad the
mouse was fast

And jumped in quickly as
the hawk flew past.

Hooray !
He made it !

There's no
place like home !

34

The fawn ran home to tell
his mother.

She said, "Some animals
catch each other."

"Some eat meat, and some eat grass.

Some are slow, and some are fast."

"A mouse can be another's meal,

And no matter how we feel,

That is Mother Nature's law !

The plan goes on without a flaw !"

The End

Saul and Paul

Vocabulary

1. Saul

2. Paul

3. August

4. fault

5. haul

6. hauling

7. autumn

8. applause

9. bēcause

au to mo bile
10. automobile

au to ma tic
11. automatic

12. Santa Claus

Saul and Paul are twins. They were seven years old in August. They hardly ever find fault with each other.

Saul and Paul have a blue wagon. They tied it to their red pedal-car.

"We can help Dad haul the leaves now," said Paul.

"Yes, I like to haul autumn leaves," said Saul.

40

Back and forth, back and forth Saul and Paul went, hauling autumn leaves.

"This is hard!" said
Paul.

"I am tired!" said Saul.
Then Saul and Paul fell
onto the big pile of
autumn leaves. Such fun
it was!

42

Just then Dad clapped
his hands.

"You two must get some
applause. You did a fine
job," he said.

"Because you are such fine kids, we have a treat for you. Get in the automobile," said Mom.

"Let's take a trip to get some ice cream," said Dad.

On the way, Saul and Paul saw a big truck. It was a leaf truck.

"Look !" yelled Paul. "There is an automatic leaf hose."

"That is what we needed," said Saul.

Dad chuckled and said, "I think I will ask Santa Claus to bring us one !" He smiled, and winked at Mom.

The End

A Play in the Basement, Bong !

Raceway
Step 25C
ing
ang
ong
ung

Vocabulary

1. gong
2. king
3. kingdom
4. bong
5. long
6. along
7. ring
8. spring
9. song
10. lungs
11. strong
12. rung
13. hung
14. bang
15. banged
16. sing
17. wing
18. hang

watch ing
19. watching

every thing
20. everything

happen ing
21. happening

Story Words

won der ful
22. wonderful

what ever
23. whatever

sud den ly
24. suddenly

an i mal
25. animal

26. again

ap pear
27. appeared

47

Last week the kids on our street gave a play. We had it in Eddy's basement.

Eddy said, "I will be the king who has a wishing ring."

Joan was the queen.
She sang a long song.
She has very strong
lungs.

49

Danny helped fix the stage. He hung a gong on the top rung of a ladder.

In the play, King Edward rubbed his wishing ring and made a wish. Danny then banged the gong with a hammer.

BONG !

Whatever King Edward wished for then appeared. First he rubbed his ring and cried, "I wish for a pretty bird to sing to me."

Danny banged on the gong.

BONG !

Suddenly a lovely bird was before the king !

52

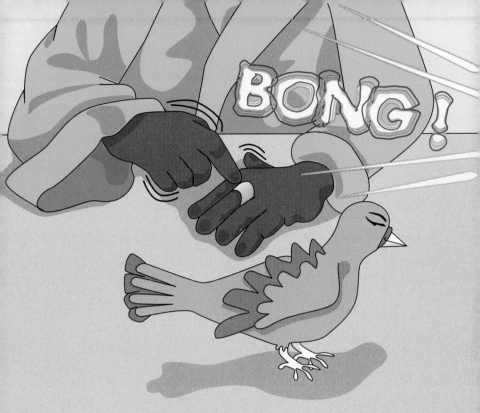

"Very well," said King Edward. "My next wish is for a wonderful animal to ride." Then he rubbed his wishing ring and again the gong went

BONG !

53

The kids pushed Willie's big dog out from under the table.

"Ahhh ! My second wish is granted," said King Edward. "A wonderful animal to ride !"

"My third wish will be for a handsome prince to marry the princess," said King Edward. "I will rub my ring once more."

BONG went the gong!

A huge frog was suddenly before the king.

"Just tell the princess to kiss this frog," said someone from under the table.

"I saw that story in a book," said a kid watching the play.

Just then the frog-prince jumped down.................... **and everything started happening !**

The lovely bird flew up! Its wing tipped King Edward's crown! His throne went toppling over and his horse ran away!

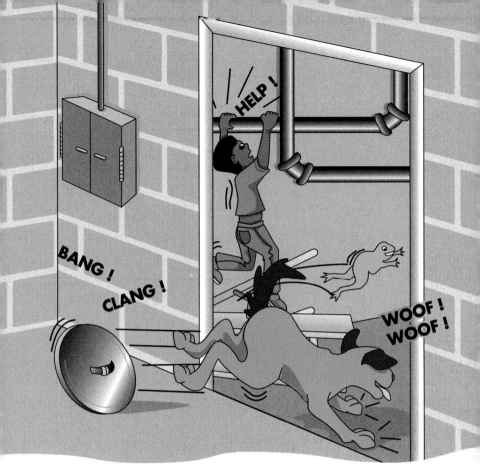

The ladder fell as the horse ran by. The gong went flying! Danny grabbed a pipe and had to hang on. It was good that he was strong!

The kids clapped and clapped. They were stamping and jumping with glee !

"We loved your show !" they said.

Yes, a play in the basement is lots of fun ! Have you ever had one ?

The End

Vocabulary

oy

1. boy
2. Roy
3. toy
4. joy
5. enjoy
6. royal
7. Joyce

oi

8. foil
9. boil
10. spoil
11. toil
12. coin
13. join
14. noise

Story Words

(ŭ)
15. covered

a lu mi num
16. aluminum

At our picnic, Mom did toil.
In a pot she began to boil
marshmallows,
chocolate,
nuts and cream.
All good things for a happy
Scout's dream.

She didn't let her candy
     stew spoil.
She covered it with
     aluminum foil.
When more Brownies came
     to join,
She gave them each a
     chocolate coin.

Roy then showed
   his wind-up toy.
It was a king we
   did enjoy.
Treats for every girl
   and boy
Made our picnic
   such a joy !
The End

His Royal Majesty

64